Giza
1924

It is 1924. You are about to join an archaeological expedition and discover a secret tomb at a site called Giza 7000X. Your guide for this journey is Will Hunt. Although Will and his family are fictitious, the rest of the information about Giza 7000X is true. It's based on the actual records—diaries, object registers, photographs, and drawings—of Dr. George Reisner, director of the Harvard University/Museum of Fine Arts, Boston, Expedition, and his team of skilled archaeologists.

Just two years earlier, in 1922, King Tut's tomb was discovered, with all its amazing treasures. Now teams of archaeologists from around the world are competing to unearth the next big archaeological find in Egypt. **Will this secret tomb be it? Whose tomb is it? And why was it hidden?**

Join Will Hunt in putting together the clues.
Can you solve this 5,000-year-old puzzle?

Illustrated by Melissa Sweet

November 15, 1924

Our King Tut Club met again today. Ever since King Tut's tomb was discovered with its gold masks, jewelry, chariots, and (my favorite, of course) King Tut's mummy, I've read everything I could about ancient Egypt. I never thought I'd have a chance to see a real pyramid or tomb, BUT my dad's been invited to work on a dig in Egypt. Will Mom and I be able to go, too?

THE 5,000-YEA

Solving a Mystery of Ancient Egypt

WITH THE COOPERATION OF THE MUSEUM OF FINE ARTS, BOSTON

Melanie Kroupa Books
Farrar · Straus · Giroux
NEW YORK

by Claudia Logan

MINUTES OF THE KING TUT CLUB
Some Things We Know About Ancient Egypt

November 15, 1924
Members present: Will, Sam

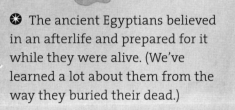

❋ The ancient Egyptians believed in an afterlife and prepared for it while they were alive. (We've learned a lot about them from the way they buried their dead.)

❋ They built tomb chambers inside or under pyramids or under rectangular structures called mastabas, or they cut them out of bedrock or cliffs.

❋ They filled these tombs with favorite belongings and things they might need—furniture, food, jewelry, clothing. They even carved and painted scenes of servants and pets to keep them company in their afterlife! (And Mom calls ME a pack rat!)

❋ They believed that a soul couldn't move on to the afterlife unless it rejoined its body, and that could happen only if the dead body didn't rot. So they figured out ways to preserve or mummify bodies.

❋ The mummy of a king, queen, or other important person was buried in a sarcophagus that was painted or carved with hieroglyphs.

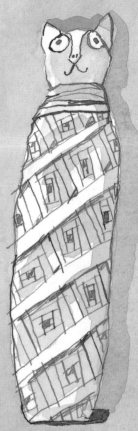

❋ Canopic jars were used to hold some of the mummy's organs, which were preserved in a natural salt called natron. (These are jars I'd definitely want to keep closed!)

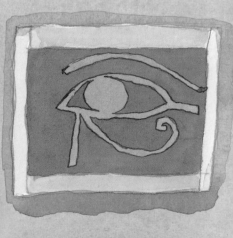

November 29, 1924

WE'RE ALL GOING! We leave in three weeks to work on Dr. George Reisner's expedition at Giza. Here's my chance to find a mummy! We'll be there for a year—maybe more. And live at Harvard Camp, right behind the pyramids, with the other archaeologists. I'll miss my friends, especially Sam, but I'm counting the days till we leave!

DR. REISNER

DR. REISNER'S TEAM

HARVARD CAMP

THE TRAVELLER'S GAZETTE.

[DECEMBER, 1924.]

RATES FOR ATLANTIC LINERS.

PASSENGERS CAN BOOK IN EITHER DIRECTION AT ANY OF COOK'S OFFICES.

(Passengers for United States must obtain U.S.A. Visa to their Passports.)

MINIMUM FARES FROM EUROPE, SUBJECT TO CHANGE.

Sphinx and pyramid, Egypt

English	Arabic	الانجليزى
dressed	labess	لابس
sewing	khyata	خياطة
cutting	tafsyl	تفصيل
in fashion	ala el moda	على الموضة
under wear	hedoom da.	هدوم داخلية
shirt	amys	قميص
breeches	labass regali	لباس رجالى
sock	shorrab	شراب
stockings	shorrab	شراب
belt	hezam	حزام
braces	hammala	حمالة
hat	borenita	برنيطة
necktie	karavatta	كرافتة
pullover	poll ovar	بول وفر
robe , gown	fostan	فستان
suit	badla	بدلة
evening dress	b sahra	بسهرة

Central Bank of Egypt
FIFTY PIASTRES
50
50

MEDITERRANEAN SEA

GIZA   CAIRO

SAKKARA

NILE RIVER

BOSTON

EGYPT

39

OFFICIAL PACKING LIST

flannel and cotton shirts
trousers and riding breeches (for riding camels?)
one pair of light boots
thin wool socks (Wool? Is our ship headed in the right direction?)
pith helmet for desert sun (Mom says I have to)
compass (so I don't get lost in the desert)
canteen (if I do get lost in the desert)
photo of Sam in Boston (if I want to see something besides the desert)
pocketknife
books (all the Sherlock Holmes mysteries I can pack)
pens and ink, stationery (postcards for Sam — I'll use our secret code)
fireball candy and my baseball cards (hard to get in Egypt!)

KING TUT CLUB CODE

Strikeout: Nothing Happening
Single: Something happening
Double: Something bigger happening
Bases Loaded: Something really big could happen
Grand Slam: MAJOR DISCOVERY!

December 5, 1924

Fourteen days till we go. It's going to take a whole month to get to the expedition site at Giza. Our ship will sail from Boston to London, then on to Alexandria. From there we take a train to Cairo. Dr. Reisner will still be working in Boston, but Dows Dunham, one of the archaeologists, will pick us up and drive us to Giza and (finally!) to Harvard Camp.

GETTING READY TO GO

WE'LL BE GONE FOR SO LONG, WE HAVE TO PACK THINGS WE CAN'T GET IN THE DESERT.

EGYPT HAS ONLY ONE INCH OF RAIN PER YEAR. IT WILL BE HOT AND SUNNY IN GIZA. NO SLEDDING!

MY FRIEND SAM WILL TAKE CARE OF MY GOLDFISH, SPHINX

ONLY 14 DAYS UNTIL WE LEAVE!

1924 DECEMBER

S	M	T	W	Th	F	S
	1	2	3	4	5	6
7	8	9	10	11	12	13
14	15	16	17	18	19	20
21	22	23	24	25	26	27
28	29	30	31			

ME

SAM

I PLAY BASEBALL AS MUCH AS I CAN — WHEN I'M NOT PACKING, THAT IS!

MY FRIENDS GIVE ME A GOOD-BYE PARTY.

I DRAW A PICTURE OF A SCARAB FOR EACH OF THEM. IT MEANS "GOOD LUCK."

your friend, Will

1924 DECEMBER

TODAY WE ARE ON OUR WAY!

SAM, WE ARE HERE

POST CARD

Dear Sam,
The travel brochure for this ship says sea air is good for your health. I say read the fine print! Now I know what "seasick" really means—I am definitely sick of the sea!
Your pal,
Will

January 3, 1925

POST C

January 7, 1925

Dear Sam,
Salaam from Alexandria! Our ship just docked. I can hardly believe my eyes—camels, jugglers, chickens, and so many people I don't know where to look! We almost missed our train because of a snake charmer.
I'll write more soon,
Will

Those Pyramids Run in the Family

I am the GREAT King Khufu, son of King Sneferu and Queen Hetep-heres. The ancient Greeks called me Cheops (Kay-ops).

My father, King Sneferu, was the first king of the Fourth Dynasty.

He built one pyramid at Maydum and two pyramids at Dahshur; one of these was the first to use the smooth pyramid shape.

But **I** built the Great Pyramid in preparation for my own burial. **MY** pyramid is the biggest one in Giza. It's amazing—481 feet high and built from 2.3 million blocks of stone. Some blocks weigh five tons — the weight of five young elephants! It took four thousand stonemasons more than twenty years to build my pyramid.

Grave Robbing

Egyptian tombs were piled high with tempting treasures. Pyramid builders tried to prevent theft by hiding entrances and creating a maze of tunnels, dead ends, and deep wells.

But tomb robbers were often the very workers who built the tombs. Transcripts of tomb robbers' court trials have been discovered on papyri and can be read today.

January 17, 1925

WE MADE IT! WE'RE HERE! Harvard Camp is right in the middle of the desert. Dad unpacks his notebooks. Mom drinks a cup of tea. But I run out to see the Great Pyramid.

A tall man wearing a long white gown comes over to me. "My name is Said Ahmed," he says, pronouncing his name "SI-yeed." He's the head of the Qufti workers on this expedition. The Quftis come from a nearby village and are trained to work with the archaeologists. He asks if I know who built the Great Pyramid.

"King Khufu," I say, glad that I've read a lot about the Egyptians.

I ask if we might find another tomb full of treasure like King Tut's, but Said just shakes his head. He says grave robbers often bribed guards to let them inside tombs, then split the treasures. An undisturbed tomb would add a lot to our knowledge of ancient Egypt. None has ever been found in Giza. But I wonder—could WE discover one?

9

The Great Royal Cemetery at Giza

The plateau of Giza, at the western edge of modern Cairo, is famous as the site of the biggest Egyptian royal tombs. There are eleven pyramids in all at Giza, built by three different pharaohs, including King Khufu. Each large pyramid has at least one small pyramid built beside it, known as the queen's pyramid or satellite pyramid.

MERAKAURE

KHAFRE

KHUFU

G7000X

WE ARE
WORKING
HERE

W S N E

January 28, 1925

Yesterday I found Dad and Mr. Dunham looking at some pieces of broken pottery. Dad showed me his notebook, called an object register. Whenever you find something, no matter how small, it gets a number and is recorded. Then you draw a picture of it, say where it was found, write what it was made of and its measurements, and tell what else was lying nearby. Dad gave me my own object register—here's what I've entered so far:

No.	DESCRIPTION	MATERIAL	MEAS.	DATE 1925	PROVENANCE	REMAR
001	candy wrapper	Paper Pinkish color	1" x 2"	Jan 27	G Street 7000	found near
002	bottle cap	metal	3/4" x 3/4	Jan 27	G Street 7000	Khufu's P
003	used matchbook	paper	2 1/2" x 1 1/2"	Jan 28		
004	piece of envelope	paper (torn	3" x 1"	Jan 28		

POST CARD

January 29, 1925

Dear Sam,
Strikeout! So much for finding Egyptian treasures. Most days I just sit around camp doing schoolwork. In the evening I talk to Said and read mysteries since there aren't any to solve here. I hope something happens—or I'm "tombed" to eternal boredom.
Your pal,
Will

February 9, 1925

Today something FINALLY happens. Said offers me a job holding the photographer's tripod. That means I'm on site at the Great Royal Cemetery with the other workers—on Queens Street, where the ancient queens are buried. I do my best to hold the tripod steady—then all of a sudden the leg collapses! What have I done? My first job—ruined.

The expedition photographer, Mohammedani Ibrahim, bends down to fix the tripod and spots some whitish plaster on the surface of the rocks. Said hurries over and calls Alan Rowe, one of the archaeologists, to have a closer look.

"This may sěem like nothing special," Said explains, "but plaster is man-made, different from other materials we find on the ground. This could mean that something is hidden below."

Hidden below! I want to grab a shovel and start digging, but Said says that the area must be cleared carefully in an orderly way.

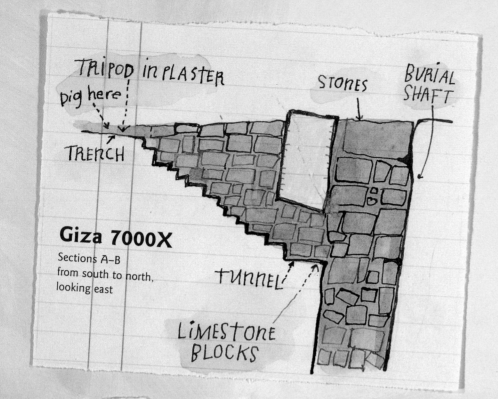

TRIPOD IN PLASTER
dig here
TRENCH
STONES
BURIAL SHAFT
TUNNEL
LIMESTONE BLOCKS

Giza 7000X

Sections A–B
from south to north,
looking east

February 23, 1925

Things are happening fast now. After the plaster has been scraped away, we find a TRENCH filled with blocks of limestone. This hides a STAIRWAY with twelve steps leading to . . . a TUNNEL! At the end of this tunnel are MORE limestone blocks set in plaster. Is this a dead end?

The excavators don't think so. They go back to Queens Street and carefully examine the area above the end of the tunnel—and they find something! A square hole cleverly filled with large unfinished stones, almost (but not quite) identical to the ones in the street.

After the stones are cleared, everyone is very excited. We have found the entrance to a SECRET PIT! Is it an undisturbed tomb?

Said looks happy. He's given me my own trowel. Time to start digging!

Tools of the Trade
An Archaeologist's Tool Kit

sieve
trowel

transit (for measuring angles)
brush

string, bags, and tags
plumb bob (for vertical level measuring)

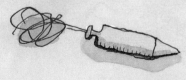

excavator's hoe

ruler and measuring tape (in centimeters)

5CM

February 25, 1925

The secret pit is a long shaft filled with all kinds of stuff—limestone chips, sand, blocks of stone, smashed bits of pottery. We keep digging down— way past the end of the blocked-up tunnel. There are notches in the wall of the shaft. Mr. Dunham says this was probably how the ancient Egyptian workmen climbed down the shaft. Suddenly I can picture them—lifting backbreaking loads up and down, day after day after day.

Workers

Life for the farmers and peasants who built pyramids could be tedious and grim. Workers hauled giant stones weighing many tons on wooden sledges across desert sands. Then they pushed these huge slabs up brick ramps where, with the help of simple levers, the stones slammed into place.

But ancient Egyptians believed that their king was a godlike figure, an expression of what was divine in their world. Like the building of cathedrals during the Middle Ages, the building of the pyramids was an important contribution to their culture.

Post Card
February 26, 1925

Dear Sam,
Guess what's happening now—week after week after week?
Here's a clue: You use a shovel.

DAY ONE
Digging

DAY TWO
More Digging

DAY THREE
Much More Digging

How much dust and plaster and limestone could there possibly be?
Answer: More than you think!
Your pal,
Will

February 27, 1925

We find a plastered area on the west wall of the shaft. Could THIS be the entrance to the burial chamber?

February 28, 1925

No luck. It's a niche in the wall, not an entrance. Inside
we find some jars that once held beer, bits of charcoal,
and the skull and three legs of an ox. Said says this was
a food offering for the dead. But where IS this dead
person? Will we ever reach his burial chamber? Said
tells me, "Don't give up. A great find could be near."

March 7, 1925

Said was right! We find the roof of the burial
chamber! Mr. Rowe removes a block of stone from
the middle of the doorway and looks in. He has
only a candle but can see a glitter of gold and the
outline of the chamber. Tomorrow he's going to go
back and get a real look at what's inside. I hope I
get to look, too!

March 8, 1925

I get up extra early today, hoping I can look in the
chamber. The workers have rigged up a basket to
lower people down the shaft. There's not a lot of
space, so no more than one or two people can go
down at once. The walls of the shaft are so fragile
that the slightest touch will make parts of them
crumble. Mr. Rowe gets the first turn. Dad, Mr.
Dunham, and the other archaeologists go down after
him, one at a time. Finally, all my begging pays off
and I get to go down, too. Here's what I see when I
look into the chamber—

a small room, the ceiling just barely high enough for a person to stand. Every single bit of space is covered with a great big jumble of stuff. It's a real mess, but it's littered with GOLD! And in the back, on top of a pile of broken pottery, there's something that looks like a gold lion's leg!

One section of the wall is covered with plaster—
I can even make out the finger marks of the mason
who smeared it thousands of years ago. I wonder
who he was. Was he afraid that he'd be entombed
down here forever?

But the most exciting thing is right up close,
underneath a tangled heap of long gold poles. It's
an alabaster sarcophagus—with its lid still on. That
means there's got to be a mummy inside! Whose
tomb IS this?

Mr. Rowe finds a clue. He spots a decorated object
and thinks he can make out King Sneferu's cartouche.
Sneferu—the father of King Khufu, who built the
Great Pyramid! Sneferu—who founded the Fourth
Dynasty of Egypt's Old Kingdom! This means our
tomb might be a thousand years older than King Tut's!

Cartouches

A cartouche is an oval ring used to
encircle the name, in hieroglyphs, of
an Egyptian king or queen. Cartouches
were either painted or carved and
resemble a coiled rope tied at one end.
A cartouche often appeared on a king's
or queen's possessions, so it can be a
useful clue for archaeologists in
identifying the owner of a particular
archaeological discovery. The cartouche
is based on the hieroglyph *shen* sign,
which is used in the word "to encircle."
This is Sneferu's cartouche.

Mr. Dunham says we must send a telegram to Dr. Reisner in Boston before we do anything else. We will send it in code so that no one will learn of our discovery!

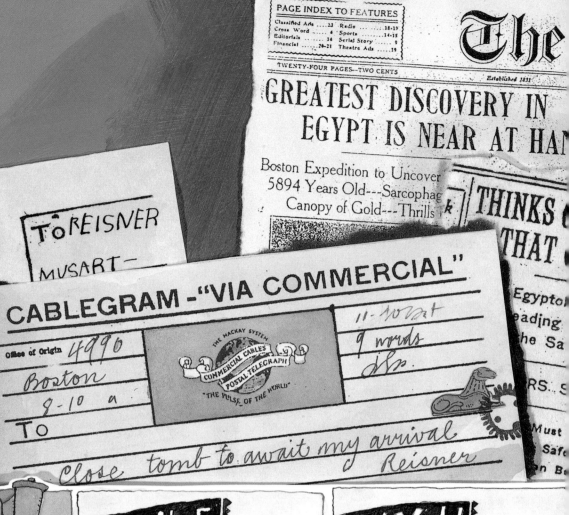

PAGE INDEX TO FEATURES
Classified Ads 13   Radio 18-19
Cross Word 4   Sports 14-15
Editorials 14   Serial Story 9
Financial 20-21   Theatre Ads 19
TWENTY-FOUR PAGES—TWO CENTS
Established 1831

The

GREATEST DISCOVERY IN EGYPT IS NEAR AT HAN...

Boston Expedition to Uncover
5894 Years Old---Sarcophag...
Canopy of Gold---Thrills...

THINKS ... THAT ...

TO REISNER
MUSART—

Harvard Camp
CAIRO.
8.13.
A Rowe
THE- NEW -PIT - 30 -METRE...
BED - WITH - REN - NESUTY - S...
SHES ... ROCK - CRUMBLING - I...
... AKHETNEBT - SO - TRA...
... FOLLOWIN...

CABLEGRAM - "VIA COMMERCIAL"
Office of Origin 4990
Boston
9-10 a
11-10 pt
9 words
Close tomb to await my arrival
Reisner

The Big Wait

MARCH 13
DR. REISNER SENDS A TELEGRAM:

TELEGRAM

CLOSE TOMB to AWAIT MY ARRIVAL

MARCH 16
REPORTERS GATHER. GUARDS ARE POSTED. THE AREA IS FENCED OFF—NO ONE IS PERMITTED to ENTER.

APRIL 5
I PLAY CHECKERS WITH SAID. (HE WINS)

MAY 4
DAD AND I GO SAILING in A FELUCCA. (HE LOSES HIS HAT OVERBOARD.)

POST CARD

EGYPTE

July 22, 1925

NEWS FLASH TO SAM!
The bases are loaded—our best hitter's on deck.
Am hoping for a grand slam!
Will

P.S. No one seems worried about the Curse of
the Pharaohs!

TOMB
NEFERU

o Decides
criptions
us

SILENT

ntil

t the

BOS

VAST TREASURES
MAY BE IN TOMB

JUNE/JULY

MOSTLY I THINK ABOUT
WHAT WE'VE FOUND:
WHY DOESN'T THIS TOMB
HAVE A PYRAMID OR MASTABA?
WAS IT MEANT TO BE HIDDEN?
DOWS DURHAM SAYS THE
SARCOPHAGUS IS ALWAYS
AT THE FAR END OF THE
BURIAL CHAMBER, WITH
FURNITURE AND PERSONAL
THINGS AT THE FRONT.
BUT IN OUR TOMB IT'S
THE OPPOSITE.
WHY?

JULY 22

FINALLY,
DR. REISNER
RETURNS!

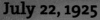

The Curse of the Pharaohs

Tombs of pharaohs were believed to be protected by a curse that said that anyone who defiled a tomb would die. By a strange coincidence, after the discovery of the tomb of King Tutankhamen in 1922, several people involved in the excavation of the tomb met with unexpected deaths, including Lord Carnarvon, who had financed the expedition. He died from an infected mosquito bite five months after the discovery.

July 22, 1925

Dr. Reisner is back! Now we can get going! Said says that it will take a long time before everything can be removed from the tomb and we find out who is in that sarcophagus. First Dr. Reisner says he wants to examine the ground around the shaft and study the excavation records. He even reads Said's diary, written in Arabic. Then seven layers of stone need to be removed before the archaeologists can see the floor of the chamber. Every layer has to be photographed and recorded, and even the smallest objects have to be drawn to scale. Removing the objects will be slow going!

Dr. Reisner's Systematic Way

1. Start with one square foot.

Looking down, draw a scale plan of this area. Include each object in its exact position.

2. Take a photograph of the area, being careful not to touch anything.

3. Carefully pick up each object on the top layer; give it a number. Then record the number in the correct position on the plan.

4. When everything visible on the first layer of the square has been removed, repeat the process for the next layer.

5. When the last layer is removed, move on to the top layer of the next square.

January 21, 1926

Today we open the tomb. Dad says, "Be quiet! Sudden noises or movements cause air currents, which can make things fall and break." I do my best, but then I start to itch and scratch. Here is a secret about this tomb: We've just opened it and already it's full of fleas!

Fleas aren't the only problem. The chamber is 100 feet underground, it's tiny, and it's so full of stuff that no one can enter without stepping on something. But Dr. Reisner says he has a way of removing and recording the exact position of every single thing in the chamber so that later he can reconstruct everything exactly as it is. It's just like a complicated puzzle.

It's really hot down here. Our glasses fog up, and the chamber's so full of dust that by the time I go back up, I'm reddish brown. But the biggest problem is it's totally dark. Can't see a thing. Then Mr. Rowe has a great idea. He sets up a mirror on the ground that reflects sunlight down to a disk plated with nickel that he's put at the bottom of the chamber. Suddenly there's light!

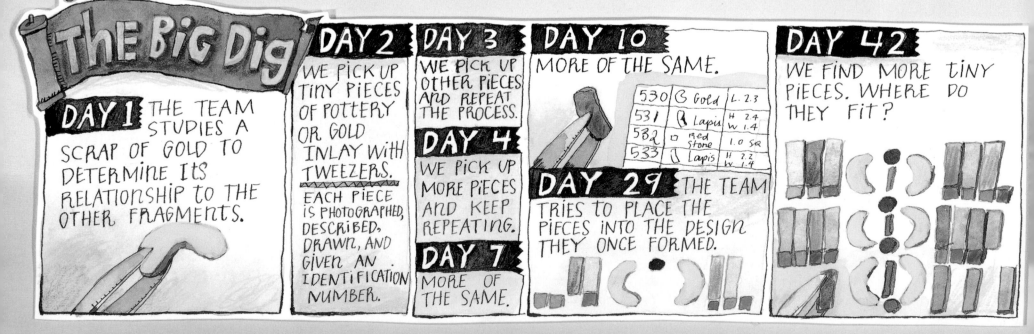

The Big Dig

DAY 1 THE TEAM STUDIES A SCRAP OF GOLD TO DETERMINE ITS RELATIONSHIP TO THE OTHER FRAGMENTS.

DAY 2 WE PICK UP TINY PIECES OF POTTERY OR GOLD INLAY WITH TWEEZERS. EACH PIECE IS PHOTOGRAPHED, DESCRIBED, DRAWN, AND GIVEN AN IDENTIFICATION NUMBER.

DAY 3 WE PICK UP OTHER PIECES AND REPEAT THE PROCESS.

DAY 4 WE PICK UP MORE PIECES AND KEEP REPEATING.

DAY 7 MORE OF THE SAME.

DAY 10 MORE OF THE SAME.

530	Gold	L. 2.3
531	Lapis	H. 2.4 W. 1.4
582	Red stone	1.0 SQ
533	Lapis	H. 2.2 W. 1.4

DAY 29 THE TEAM TRIES TO PLACE THE PIECES INTO THE DESIGN THEY ONCE FORMED.

DAY 42 WE FIND MORE TINY PIECES. WHERE DO THEY FIT?

February 6, 1926

Dear Sam,
It's not easy being an archaeologist. Or even a lowly helper. No air, no light, lots of dust and FLEAS! What are we doing? Picking up things hour after hour with TWEEZERS. If some- one sneezes or trips—there goes 5,000 years of history down the drain. And I don't want to spend another 5,000 years putting things back together!
Your VERY careful pal,
Will

POST CARD

Dear Sam,
February 8, 1926
Flea problem solved! Take sheets of flypaper. Spread them out across the tomb at the end of the day. Return next morning to count fleas (the systematic way, of course!). No more scratching—
Will

February 9, 1926

Trouble today. Said is ill. He's been taken to the hospital in Old Cairo. Dr. Reisner tells us that he has pneumonia.

Qufti Workers

The professional diggers at Harvard Camp all came from a few large, extended families in the Egyptian village of Quft. For generations, these families worked on archaeological digs. As Qufti boys came of age, fathers and uncles recommended them as workers. The Quftis were excellent excavators, so honest that it was unheard of for an artifact to be stolen. The reputation of each family—and its livelihood—depended on the conduct of each family worker.

February 15, 1926

Something terrible has happened. Dr. Reisner calls us all together and says that Said has died. All is quiet. Then some of the Qufti workers from Said's village begin to make a noise, not like singing, more like wailing. Mr. Dunham says this is what Quftis do to mourn.

There are five thousand people at Said's funeral. I look at Mom and Dad and I feel like crying. Dr. Reisner talks about how in 1899 Said came to the expedition as a small boy to carry his camera and notebooks. For twenty-seven years Said has been like a son to him, helping him make many discoveries at Giza. Dr. Reisner says that the best way to honor Said is to keep working. We must solve the mystery of whose tomb this is. For Said.

February 18, 1926

Today Dr. Reisner invites me to his office. He has mystery books piled everywhere. "Being an archaeologist is a lot like being a detective," he says. "You can't force the evidence to fit your ideas." Then he asks me who I think the owner of the tomb is.

"Sneferu," I say, remembering the cartouche.

But Dr. Reisner tells me that I need to look at the whole picture. He tells me to keep paying attention to every detail. Then he hands me a book of detective stories—starring Sherlock Holmes, of course.

March 1, 1926

I keep my eyes open. Today we discover a possible new clue: The sarcophagus is chipped. There are pieces missing from the box and the lid. What does that mean?

Dr. Reisner says that the gold sheets and bars we've found were once part of furniture. Wood rots, but gold lasts forever. Everyone is excited—no furniture from the Old Kingdom has ever been found. Dr. Reisner identifies the first piece of furniture—a carrying chair. Gold designs and hieroglyphs were inlaid into ebony panels. Now the ebony is gone, but the gold remains in the same position it was placed five thousand years ago!

The archaeologists take tweezers to lift one tiny inlay piece after another without disturbing those around it—laying the pieces out on trays in their original order so that we can reconstruct the designs.

If we can decipher the hieroglyphs on the chair, will they tell us who the owner of the tomb is? That owner—and the answer—is lying in the sarcophagus. Mr. Dunham says that, because of its position among all the other artifacts, the sarcophagus will be the last object to be opened. To make certain that no one disturbs it, Dr. Reisner has secured the lid of the sarcophagus with mud-and-paper seals.

I start drawing everything that comes up out of the tomb in my object register.

ON	MATERIAL	MEAS.	DATE 1926	PROVENANCE	REMARKS
	gold	W2 W.1	Mar. 1	G Street 7000	
r	limestone		Mar. 1	G Street 7000	
	gold	1½ × 1¾	Mar. 1	G Street 7000	molded with lines on both sides

March 9, 1926

Mr. Dunham, Dad, and the others are working on the gold hieroglyphs. The back of each hieroglyph is supposed to be smooth, but bits of gold were gouged out before each piece was put into place. Mr. Dunham says we've discovered a crime by the clever craftsman who made this chair five thousand years ago. The hieroglyphs are in really bad shape—almost impossible to read—but if we can decipher them, it could reveal the owner of the tomb. Mr. Dunham lets me copy the hieroglyphic symbols from his notebook so I can try, too.

Hieroglyphs

Ancient Egyptian hieroglyphic writing is made up of over eight hundred different characters. Many represent concepts (just as the modern character $ stands for money), but the hieroglyphs shown here stand for the sounds represented by the letters of our alphabet. In writing proper names, a masculine name is followed by the hieroglyph of a seated man, a female name by the hieroglyph of a seated woman. Hieroglyphs can be written either vertically or horizontally.

Post Card

April 14, 1926

Dear

For weeks, instead of doing my schoolwork, I've been trying to figure out these hieroglyphs—but Mr. Dunham beat me to it! Now we know! GRAND SLAM! Your pal,

25

Translation:

MOTHER OF THE
KING OF UPPER
AND LOWER
EGYPT,

❋

FOLLOWER OF
HORUS,

❋

GUIDE OF THE
RULER,

❋

FAVORITE ONE,

❋

SHE WHOSE
EVERY WORD IS
DONE FOR HER,

❋

THE DAUGHTER
OF THE GOD'S
BODY,

❋

HETEP-HERES

WONDERS OF EGYPT 6,000 YEARS AGO.

Tomb of the Mother of Famous Pharaoh.

INSCRIPTIONS IN GOLD.

Wonderful descriptions of the handiwork of the royal artificers of Egypt 6,000 years ago are given by Dr. Reisner, of Chicago, who has been exploring the tomb of Queen Hetepheres, mother of Cheops, the builder of the Greatest Pyramid.

Golden inscriptions prove the accuracy of the earlier deductions and the great archœological value of these discoveries.

Queen Hetepheres died soon after her son (Khufu) came to the Throne.

RESURRECTIONISTS IN QUEEN'S TOMB.

How Royal Pyramid-Builder Saved Mother's Remains.

CAIRO, Tuesday.

FIND
OF

First
Discussi
d:
Every
tulate
gyptia
nt:
y to
ouch
s
Sr
is

GOLD
IN A

Discoverer

April 16, 1926

So one mystery is solved: The tomb belongs to Queen Hetep-heres, wife of Sneferu and mother of King Khufu, who built the Great Pyramid. But there are still questions. If this was a tomb of a famous queen, why was it hidden? Why is it such a mess—with everything put into it in the wrong order? The answer must lie in the sarcophagus.

September 23, 1926

It's wait, wait, wait for the sarcophagus. Everyone is still busy—there are other finds to be examined and pieced together. Near the sarcophagus are the remains of a chest that once held the queen's special things. And one of those is a jewelry box sheathed in gold! Inside are two rows of silver bracelets (twenty of them) studded with turquoise and other stones. Dr. Reisner thinks the queen wore these as anklets.

Anklets or Bracelets?

One of the expedition's most exciting discoveries was the queen's jewelry box, mostly disintegrated but with many of its sheets of gold casing still intact. In the midst of these sheets lay two sets of ten silver rings, graded in size from smaller to larger. Each ring was inlaid with semiprecious stones in a butterfly design.

At first Dr. Reisner thought these big rings were anklets. But the team later discovered in the tomb a representation of the queen wearing these very rings from her wrists to her forearms—confirming them to be bracelets.

POST CARD

September 25, 1926

Dear Sam,
More delays. Dr. Reisner's been sick and the opening of the sarcophagus postponed. I'm beginning to believe in that curse. My mom says I need to be patient—the mummy's not going anywhere. It's already been here a few thousand years. I'll be ancient myself by the time we open the sarcophagus!
Your old pal,
Will

27

POST CARD

Dear Sam,

October 1, 1926

I actually touched some of the queen's things today. First I put on special linen gloves and then Mr. Dunham let me pick up a gold cup, a tiny copper needle, and even a small gold tool the queen used for cleaning her nails. Seeing and touching her things makes her seem like a real person. It's strange to think she lived almost 5,000 years ago. If someone found my baseball glove 5,000 years from now, what would they think of me?

Will

October 15, 1926

More discoveries. And more mysteries!

Things are a mess in this tomb. After thousands of years, the wooden carrying boxes disintegrated, and everything inside is in a mixed-up heap. But other things seem mixed up, too.

We already know that the sarcophagus was chipped. But now some of the chips have been found across the chamber with the broken pottery! A gold cup was discovered there, too, separated from a matching saucer found with the queen's special things!

The pottery is a broken jumble, but Dr. Reisner is certain that it was broken BEFORE it was packed—the pieces from one kind of pottery are all mixed up with pieces of a DIFFERENT kind of pottery.

What's going on here? This is a queen's tomb, but it seems like everything was just thrown in. Will everything become clear when we FINALLY open the sarcophagus?

March 3, 1927

TODAY'S THE DAY! We'll finally find out who's in that tomb. Dr. Reisner has invited the American ambassador and other important people to watch us open the sarcophagus. Now there's an armchair instead of a basket to carry people down to the chamber. "Luxury accommodations," my mom says. I can hardly wait!

Giza Pyramids, March

I, the undersigned, being about to be admitted to the tomb G 7000 X, have been warned of the possible danger to life and limb arising from accidents during the ascent and descent, and I accept personally all responsibility for damage resulting to myself from said admission.

I also agree, in accordance with the regulations of the Egyptian Government Authorities, that no interview or news concerning the tomb G 7000 X shall be given out by me to the daily press or to any weekly, monthly or other periodical, or to any agents thereof, or shall be utilized by me for any publication whatever until after the scientific publication of the tomb.

L. R. Taylor

Mr. Dunham and another man stand ready to
turn the jacks to lift the lid. Dr. Reisner gives a
nod. A crack appears between the lid and the
box. Little by little it widens until we can see
the upper part of the box. Everyone peers inside.

IT'S A DUD! An empty sarcophagus! So much for the mummy that wasn't going anywhere.

"It appears that Queen Hetep-heres is not receiving today," says Dr. Reisner. He invites everyone back to Harvard Camp for cake and then turns to look at the plastered niche in the wall above the sarcophagus. What lies behind it?

May 23, 1927

Finally, they clear out the niche. Guess what? It's not the mummy but a plain, square alabaster box with Queen Hetep-heres's hieroglyphs on it. It's her canopic chest. There are no canopic jars, but inside, in four compartments, are the queen's INTESTINES, STOMACH, LUNGS, and LIVER! Dr. Reisner says, "I'm afraid this is all that remains of King Khufu's mother."

But even this is amazing. It's been five thousand years and here are her organs! There's still liquid natron in two of the compartments. This is the first time natron has EVER been discovered. "Now we have absolute proof that this was Queen Hetep-heres's tomb," Dr. Reisner says. Then he looks at me. "A mummy is missing from a sealed tomb. This is probably the kind of mystery you like."

He's right. But will we be able to solve it before I go home?

What SHOULD Have Happened to Queen Hetep-heres
How the Ancient Egyptians Buried Their Dead

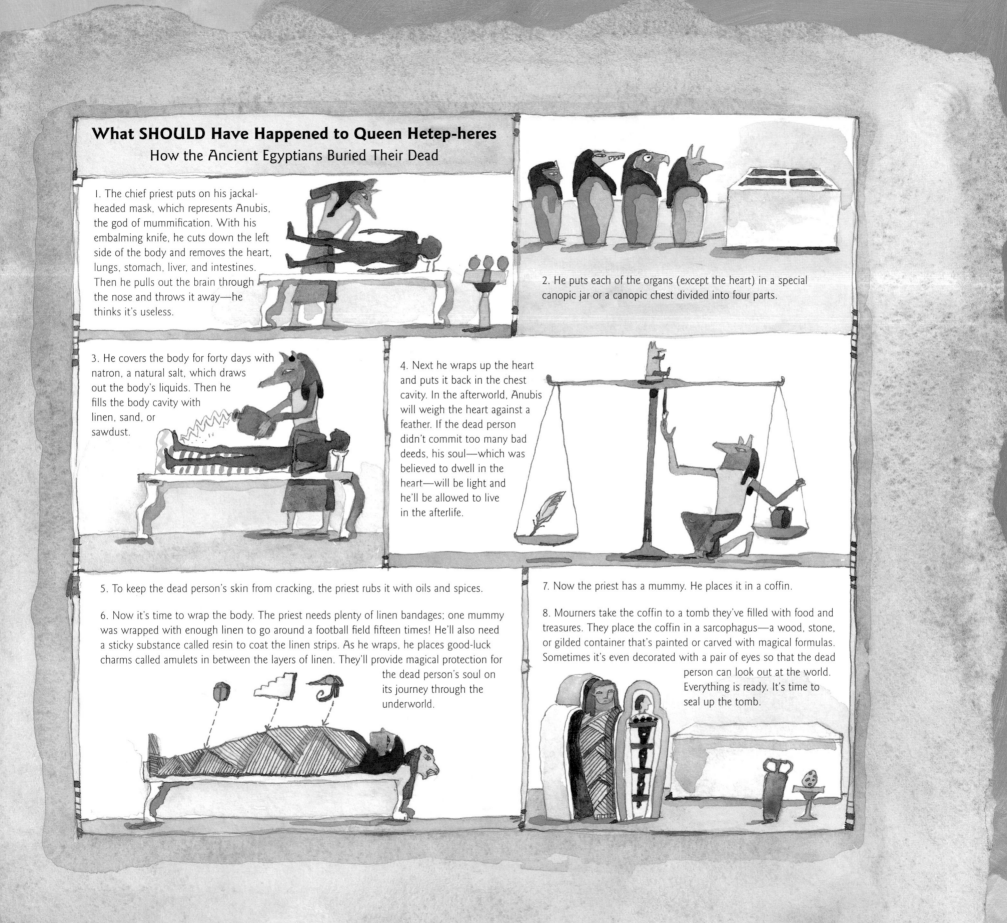

1. The chief priest puts on his jackal-headed mask, which represents Anubis, the god of mummification. With his embalming knife, he cuts down the left side of the body and removes the heart, lungs, stomach, liver, and intestines. Then he pulls out the brain through the nose and throws it away—he thinks it's useless.

2. He puts each of the organs (except the heart) in a special canopic jar or a canopic chest divided into four parts.

3. He covers the body for forty days with natron, a natural salt, which draws out the body's liquids. Then he fills the body cavity with linen, sand, or sawdust.

4. Next he wraps up the heart and puts it back in the chest cavity. In the afterworld, Anubis will weigh the heart against a feather. If the dead person didn't commit too many bad deeds, his soul—which was believed to dwell in the heart—will be light and he'll be allowed to live in the afterlife.

5. To keep the dead person's skin from cracking, the priest rubs it with oils and spices.

6. Now it's time to wrap the body. The priest needs plenty of linen bandages; one mummy was wrapped with enough linen to go around a football field fifteen times! He'll also need a sticky substance called resin to coat the linen strips. As he wraps, he places good-luck charms called amulets in between the layers of linen. They'll provide magical protection for the dead person's soul on its journey through the underworld.

7. Now the priest has a mummy. He places it in a coffin.

8. Mourners take the coffin to a tomb they've filled with food and treasures. They place the coffin in a sarcophagus—a wood, stone, or gilded container that's painted or carved with magical formulas. Sometimes it's even decorated with a pair of eyes so that the dead person can look out at the world. Everything is ready. It's time to seal up the tomb.

Post Card   May 25, 1927

Dear Sam,
Only a few weeks until I leave and we STILL haven't solved this
mystery. With the discovery of the canopic chest, we now have
everything from the tomb—except the mummy (of "corpse").
Dr. Reisner says this is the real work of an archaeologist—trying
to solve a mystery that happened thousands of years
ago. But I think even Sherlock Holmes might be
stumped by this one!
Will

P.S. Tell Sphinx I'll be home soon.

May 25, 1927

CLUES:

1. **Tomb is hidden**—a secret tomb. No pyramid or mastaba on top. Why?

2. **Tomb is sealed**—no one could have gotten in—but the queen is missing! Would Egyptians bury an empty sarcophagus? Never!

3. **Burial chamber a mess!** (Things fall apart after thousands of years, but they don't move to the wrong places.)

4. **Pottery broken *before* placed in tomb**. Why?

5. **Sarcophagus (and lid) is chipped**—did someone pry it open? (How could they have gotten into a SEALED tomb? And if they did, why didn't they take the gold?)

6. **Chips from sarcophagus found mixed in with broken pottery**. Why?

7. **But—food offering and canopic chest are undisturbed.**

8. **And everything placed in tomb in reverse order.** Why??? How??? Who???

Said told me, "Don't give up."
I *will* solve this mystery!

June 15, 1927

We are leaving in a few days. I go to see Dr. Reisner to return his mystery books and I ask him, "Could someone have gotten inside? Could it have been grave robbers?"

He smiles and says, "Congratulations! You've uncovered one piece of our puzzle." He thinks there WERE grave robbers—they just didn't rob *this* grave! This is what he tells me:

DR. REISNER'S THEORY

During the reign of the great King Khufu, while everyone's attention was focused on the new royal cemetery at Giza and the construction of the Great Pyramid, the old cemetery at Dahshur was left to the care of guards and funerary priests. I believe that Queen Hetep-heres was originally entombed at Dahshur and that the temptation of her gold inspired an evil conspiracy.

Somehow thieves—possibly including some of the very masons and quarrymen who had prepared Queen Hetep-heres's tomb—stole into the tomb at night, lighting their way with torches. They must have been in a terrible hurry, throwing objects about the room, breaking pottery, trampling whatever was underfoot, for they didn't bother to strip the gold casings from the furniture or to search the rest of the burial deposit—but made straight for the sarcophagus, where the most valuable objects could be found. The lid of the sarcophagus was difficult to open, so they used metal chisels to pry it up, breaking off one corner and chipping both lid and box.

They dragged the queen's body out where they could strip off the linen wrappings to search for gold ornaments concealed in the folds of cloth. Her head and limbs would have been broken off so that they could remove the necklaces, bracelets, and anklets that she was wearing, and her remains would have been left for jackals.

This robbery would not have gone unnoticed. A report would have gone straight to King Khufu's chief vizier, who would know at once that he and all his party at court were in great danger—a sacred tomb had been violated! To conceal the destruction of the queen's mummy from King Khufu, he would have placed the chipped lid back on the sarcophagus and arrested every person who could possibly have known the truth.

To draw attention away from the robbery at Dahshur, the vizier himself may have suggested that the queen's burial would be safer beside the king's own pyramid at Giza. No one would have dared look inside the sarcophagus before it was transported to Giza along with the remaining contents of her tomb—the broken pottery packed in new wooden boxes to conceal the damage.

The vizier would have been in a great hurry to seal up his secret, so he wouldn't have bothered with the usual careful placement of objects in the new tomb. When everything was in the chamber, workmen simply filled in the shaft. Then they craftily set blocks of local stone on top to look like the surrounding surface of rock.

And Queen Hetep-heres, or what was left of her in her canopic chest, remained undisturbed until our discovery, quite by accident—five thousand years later.

June 17, 1927

POST CARD

Dear Sam,
Time to go. We leave for Cairo tomorrow. I'll miss Harvard Camp,
Dr. Reisner, Mr. Dunham, the workers, even the fleas. We've found
some real treasures, like the queen's jewelry box, but I know that
what we've learned is just as important as any treasure we might
have uncovered. Said was right. Archaeology takes time—no matter
how much you want something to happen. He said we were on the
verge of "a great find," and he was right about that, too. We have one
answer to the mystery of this secret tomb. But is it the whole story?
Your soon-to-be-seasick pal,
Will

MY FRIEND, SAID, WITH HIS SON

No.	DESCRIPTION	MATERIAL	MEAS.	DATE	PROVENANCE	REMARKS
7001	lion's leg	wood/gold	21" x 5"	June 30	G. Street 7000	wood has rotten
7002	bracelet	silver and stones	4" in diam.	July 1	G. Street 7000	only gold remain
7003	coin	copper	1"	July 1	G. Street 7000	some stones are missing
7004	stone	lapis	1/4"	July 1	G. Street 7000	

Facts About Giza 7000X

Queen Hetep-heres's secret tomb is the oldest undisturbed royal burial ever found in Egypt. It revealed some of the finest examples of Egyptian furniture and jewelry from the Old Kingdom.

Major finds include:

queen's carrying chair of cedarwood and ebony, inlaid with gold hieroglyphs

cedarwood armchair trimmed in heavily beaten gold

queen's bed, sheathed in gold, supported by four gold-sheathed lion's legs

canopy for the queen's bed with the names and titles of King Sneferu on it

box with gold and inlay work that once held curtains for the queen's bed

two sets of silver bracelets inlaid with semiprecious stones in a butterfly motif

queen's jewelry box

alabaster sarcophagus

alabaster canopic chest with the remains of the queen's organs

thirty alabaster vessels; large copper pitcher with copper basin; gold drinking cup; two gold saucers; gold razors, knives, and manicure implements; copper razors and knives; copper tools; copper needle; toiletry box with eight alabaster ointment jars and copper spoon

Giza 7000X involved 321 working days, 1,057 photographs, and more than 1,700 pages of notes and drawings that became a permanent record of the work. Dr. Reisner was the first archaeologist to make fully systematic excavations in Egypt and the first to document every step of expedition work with photographs. It is only because every move of the dig was meticulously recorded that it was possible to make exact reconstructions of the ancient furniture found. The original pieces are now in the Egyptian Museum in Cairo, and accurate reproductions are on exhibit at the Museum of Fine Arts in Boston.

RAISING THE SARCOPHAGUS

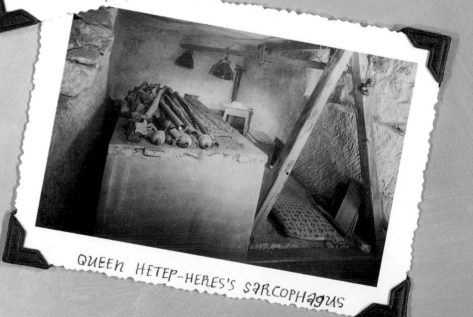

AT WORK IN THE TOMB

QUEEN HETEP-HERES'S SARCOPHAGUS

New Tools of the Trade

* computerized surveying equipment, called total stations

* computers with drawing software and databases to keep track of finds and their documentation

* scanners for entering photos and drawings into the computer databases

* magnetic resistivity surveying equipment to detect subterranean features without excavating

* digital cameras (for instant on-site documentation)

Of course, many of the classic archaeologist's tools are still used as well, including trowels, brushes, baskets for removing earth, sieves, measuring tapes, rulers, string, bags, and tags. Modern digs also involve the cooperation of various interdisciplinary specialists, including botanists, zoologists, geologists, sedimentologists, photographers, draftspeople, architects, Egyptologists, and technical support staff.

Another Theory About the Missing Queen

Like detectives, archaeologists use clues to uncover the truth, but unlike mysteries, archaeological discoveries rarely end with one solution. Building on earlier records and the discoveries of the past but using new tools and technology, archaeologists today continue to unearth new discoveries as well as to explore new theories about earlier finds such as Giza 7000X.

Dr. Mark Lehner, an archaeologist from the University of Chicago, has researched the Hetep-heres puzzle and offers a theory that differs from Dr. Reisner's. He suggests that Queen Hetep-heres's body is missing because it was reburied in one of the three queens' pyramids that King Khufu had built near his own Great Pyramid. The mortuary chapels of two of these queens' pyramids have been completely destroyed by robbers, so no one can be certain who they were intended for. But given the burial customs of the time, the fact that one of the three queens' pyramids is perfectly aligned with a satellite pyramid of King Khufu suggests that Queen Hetep-heres might have been reburied there.

Could the mystery of the missing queen be due to a change in building plans? Was her body simply removed and buried in a new sarcophagus with a new set of possessions? And if it was, how does one explain the fact that everything in her tomb, Giza 7000X, was placed in reverse order?

Dr. Lehner suggests that the truth may lie somewhere between his explanation and that of Dr. Reisner. Since only 15 percent of Giza has been excavated to date, there still may be many more exciting discoveries and theories to come.

For Peggy Burchenal and Peggy Hogan

And for Melanie—
the most patient editor in the history of the breed
C.L.

For Cabbit
M.S.

✹

ACKNOWLEDGMENTS

The author would like to gratefully acknowledge the role of the Museum of Fine Arts, Boston, in the creation of this book. Materials such as diary entries, object register notations, photographs, and drawings, as well as other archival materials, were generously made available through the Department of Art of the Ancient World. Throughout the development of the book we have relied on the help of Peter Der Manuelian, Mellon Research Fellow in Egyptian Art, to answer questions, to explain obscure and difficult archaeological and historical facts, and to provide a vigilant eye for accuracy. It would have been impossible to retell this fascinating story without Dr. Manuelian's help. His wonderful sense of humor and ability to translate the most scholarly fact into an interesting and understandable explanation were essential in helping turn the museum's fifty boxes of expedition records and facts into a book.

This book was truly a collaboration and would not have been possible without a great deal of help that came in a variety of forms: in no particular order, my husband, Chris Logan, and my children, Ben and Otti, for being everything; Terri Schmitz, my unofficial editor on paper and off; Abby Rordorf, Polly Horvath, Alice Lucey, Sharon McBride, Virginia Evans, Nina Schwartz, Kathy and David Coen, and the staff of The Children's Book Shop in Brookline; the 72 Huron Bus & 02140 Committee; and, most of all, the students and colleagues I worked with from my teaching days, who showed me what a real expedition could be.

Text copyright © 2002 by Claudia Logan
Illustrations copyright © 2002 by Melissa Sweet
All rights reserved
Photographs courtesy Museum of Fine Arts, Boston. Reproduced with permission
Copyright © 2000 Museum of Fine Arts, Boston
All rights reserved
Distributed in Canada by Douglas & McIntyre Ltd.
Color separations by Bright Arts (H.K.) Ltd.
Printed and bound in Hong Kong by South China Printing Company (1988) Ltd.
Book design by Virginia Evans
The illustrations for this book were created in acrylic and watercolor.
First edition, 2002
10 9 8 7 6 5 4 3 2 1

Library of Congress Cataloging-in-Publication Data
Logan, Claudia.
   The 5,000-year-old puzzle : solving a mystery of ancient Egypt / by Claudia Logan ; illustrated by Melissa Sweet.— 1st ed.
      p. cm.
   Summary: An account of Dr. George Reisner's 1925 discovery and excavation of a secret tomb in Giza, Egypt, based on archival documents and records, but told through the fictionalized experiences of a young boy who accompanies his father on the dig.
   ISBN 0-374-32335-6
   1. Jîzah (Egypt)—Antiquities—Juvenile fiction. 2. Tombs—Egypt—Juvenile fiction. [1. Jîzah (Egypt)—Antiquities—Fiction. 2. Tombs—Egypt—Fiction. 3. Archaeology—Fiction.]
I. Title: Five-thousand-year-old puzzle. II. Sweet, Melissa, ill. III. Title.

PZ7.L82765 Aad 2001
[Fic]—dc21   00-60243